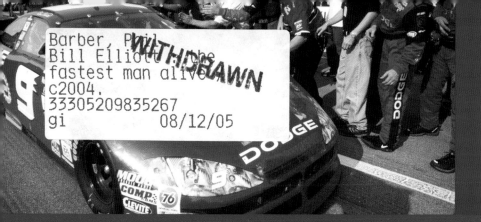

THE WORLD OF NASCAR

BILL ELLIOTT: The Fastest Man Alive

BY PHIL BARBER

T R A D I T I O N   B O O K S ®
A New Tradition in Children's Publishing™
M A P L E   P L A I N

Published by **Tradition Books**® and distributed to the
school and library market by **The Child's World**®
P.O. Box 326
Chanhassen, MN 55317-0326
800/599-READ
http://www.childsworld.com

Photo Credits
Cover: Sports Gallery: Al Messerschmidt (top), Brian Spurlock (bottom)
AP/Wide World: 5, 6
Corbis: 13, 14, 20
Dick Conway: 8, 9, 10, 11, 16
Getty Images: 19, 23, 28
Sports Gallery: 15, 18, 21, 27 (Al Messerschmidt), 24, (Brian Spurlock)

An Editorial Directions book
Editorial Directions, Inc.: E. Russell Primm, Editorial Director; Katie Marsico and Elizabeth K.
Martin, Assistant Editors; Olivia Nellums, Editorial Assistant; Susan Hindman, Copy Editor;
Susan Ashley, Proofreader; Kevin Cunningham, Fact Checker; Tim Griffin/IndexServ, Indexer;
James Buckley Jr., Photo Researcher and Selector

The Design Lab: Kathy Petelinsek, Art Director and Designer; Kari Thornborough,
Page Production

Library of Congress Cataloging-in-Publication Data
Barber, Phil.
  Bill Elliott : the fastest man alive / by Phil Barber.
    p. cm. — (The world of NASCAR series)
Includes index.
Summary: A simple biography of NASCAR championship driver, Bill Elliott.
  ISBN 1-59187-026-7 (lib. bdg. : alk. paper)
  1. Elliott, Bill, 1955– —Juvenile literature. 2. Automobile racing drivers—United States—
Biography—Juvenile literature. [1. Elliott, Bill, 1955– 2. Automobile racing drivers.] I. Title. II.
Series.
  GV1032.E44 B37 2004
  796.72'092—dc21   2003004992

Note: Beginning with the 2004 season, the NASCAR
Winston Cup Series will be called the NASCAR Nextel
Cup Series.

BILL ELLIOTT

Table of Contents

4   **Introduction:** Built for Speed

7   **Chapter One:** Awesome Bill from Dawsonville

12   **Chapter Two:** Decade of Dominance

17   **Chapter Three:** End of a Drought

22   **Chapter Four:** Second Childhood

29   Bill Elliott's Life

30   Glossary

31   For More Information about Bill Elliott

32   Index

I N T R O D U C T I O N

Built for Speed

few NASCAR drivers have won more races than Bill Elliott. There probably have been better **strategists** and guys who were more skillful at passing or cornering. But no one has ever driven a stock car faster than the man they call Million Dollar Bill. Maybe that's why so many thousands of NASCAR fans have turned out to see him over the years.

The first hint of Bill's speed came on February 9, 1985, when he won the **pole position** at the Daytona 500. Bill was 29 years old and already had won a few races. But this was Daytona, the granddaddy of them all. When his speedometer hit 205.114 miles (330 kilometers) per hour in his qualifying run, the racing world took notice. That wouldn't be the only pole captured by Bill Elliott. In the last 20 years, only Darrell Waltrip has been out front more.

Among Bill's many blurry runs, one qualifying lap stands above the rest. It was at Talladega Speedway in 1987. When the **green flag** waved, Bill had the gas pedal of his No. 9 car floored. He cut the first turn sharp, rocketed through the straightaway, hit another crisp turn and came out flying! Gravity tugged at Bill, and the vibration of the car made it hard to see clearly, but he ran a perfect circuit.

After winning the 1985 Daytona 500, Bill Elliott celebrated with his wife Martha and his very happy daughter Starr (in helmet).

When they posted his time at Talladega, the crowd was stunned. Bill had done his lap at 212.809 miles (342.4 km) per hour. No one, before or since, has recorded a faster speed. Now NASCAR has added **restrictor plates** to cars at **super-speedways,** hoping to reduce dangerous crashes. So there's a chance Bill's record will never be broken.

Bill Elliott drove this car faster than any other man in NASCAR history, topping 212 miles (342 km) per hour in 1987.

C H A P T E R   O N E

Awesome Bill from Dawsonville

There wasn't a lot of entertainment for kids growing up in Dawsonville, Georgia, population 550. Teenagers liked to fix up old Chevys and Dodges and race up and down Georgia State Highway 9, the old "Whiskey Trail" that **bootleggers** followed in the 1930s.

George Elliott knew all about driving. When he was a boy, one of his good friends was Gober Sosebee, one of NASCAR's earliest winners. He also knew Lloyd Seay and Roy Hall, two legendary drivers from before the birth of NASCAR.

George figured his sons—Ernie, Dan, and Bill—would wind up behind the wheel. He encouraged them to get into

organized racing. It was Bill, the youngest, who finally took him up on it.

Bill didn't explode into stardom right away. He spent a long time in the Sportsman division, until George fixed up an old Ford Torino and set his sights on the Winston Cup. On February 29, 1976, Bill entered his first NASCAR event at North Carolina Speedway at the age of 21. His car was No. 9, a tribute to the old highway that ran through Dawsonville. He didn't win. In fact, the young driver ran eight Winston Cup races that year and finished only two of them. But his time was coming.

That's Bill on the right, zooming around the track during a Late Model Sportsman race.

In 1977, one of NASCAR's most successful teams—owner Roger Penske and driver Bobby Allison—went their separate ways. Penske decided to sell his racing equipment to George Elliott. Now Bill had a top-flight ride. But the Elliotts still ran a small operation, with practically no outside sponsorship.

In 1979, Bill made a small splash when he finished second to legendary David Pearson in the Southern 500 at Darlington Raceway in South Carolina. After the race, you would have thought Bill had won. He grinned from ear to ear and told reporters, "Maaan, I'm proud!" They loved this friendly young driver, and soon the fans would, too.

Bill was still looking for his big breakthrough, and it came in 1983. That's the year Michigan businessman Harry Melling

Bill's brother, Ernie, has always been a key part of his team. Above, he is watching from the pits during a 1983 race.

bought the operation from George. The garage would remain in Georgia, with Ernie Elliott in charge of the engine room and Bill looking after the **chassis.** But now the team had plenty of money for hiring crew members and maintaining the car.

Money can't win races by itself, but it sure helps. Soon after signing with Melling, Bill got his first NASCAR win at the Winston Western 500 in Riverside, California. It had taken him 117 starts, but he finally took a **checkered flag.** Some called it a fluke, but the Elliotts knew better.

Look for the name of Elliott's new car owner on the side of the No. 9 car as its crew hustles through a pit stop in 1983.

MY THREE SONS

Despite their father's encouragement, the Elliott brothers were reluctant racers. Ernie tried his hand at some short-track racing in Georgia and gave it up. Dan said, "Forget it." The "baby" finally got his chance one night at Dixie Speedway, north of Atlanta. Bill was green, but he drove a pretty strong race for a first-timer. As the story goes, when Bill finished, Ernie turned to George and said, "Daddy, there's your driver."

Who's this kid? A very young Bill Elliott pauses for a soda before the start of his first Winston Cup race in 1976.

C H A P T E R   T W O

Decade of Dominance

When Bill Elliott and Harry Melling became partners in 1983, it marked the beginning of an amazing run. From 1983 to 1994, Bill finished out of the top 10 in the Winston Cup point standings only once. He won 40 races in those 12 years, including twice at Daytona. He won an unprecedented 11 superspeedway races in 1985 and was the Winston Cup champion in 1988. In 1992, he won four consecutive races to tie the modern-day record.

Part of the reason for Bill's success was his fearless, all-out driving style. Another reason was his mechanical knowledge. Some drivers are hands-off, leaving the wrenches and oil cans to their crews. But Bill spent a lot of time under the hood with his dad when he was a boy.

"He worked on the car just like a regular crew member,"

fellow top driver Darrell Waltrip once said. "That's a real asset. He knows when the car's not right, and he knows how to make it right."

As the victories mounted for Bill, so did the honors. In 1985, he was the first Winston Cup driver ever to appear on the cover of *Sports Illustrated*. In 1998, he was named one of NASCAR's 50 Greatest Drivers of All Time. That same year, he was inducted into the Georgia Sports Hall of Fame, joining athletes such as baseball legend Ty Cobb and football player Herschel Walker.

The checkered flag drops and Bill crosses the finish line as the winner of the 1987 Daytona 500.

In addition, in a fan poll conducted by *ESPN Speedweek,* Bill was named Driver of the Decade for the 1990s. That, of course, was no surprise. Few stock-car drivers ever have drawn more fan support than Bill Elliott.

How popular is he? Since 1956, NASCAR has awarded an annual trophy to its Most Popular Driver. Bill has won the award 16 times, far more than any other driver. The great

Bill kicked off his great success in the 1990s by winning this race at Dover Downs Speedway in 1990.

Richard Petty ranks second, with nine trophies. In fact, some race fans feel that when Bill finally retires one day, NASCAR should rename this prize the Bill Elliott Trophy.

It isn't hard to figure out why Bill is so loved in the race community. First of all, he's a heck of a driver. He's also involved with several charities, including the Special Olympics, the M.D.

Anderson Cancer Center, and the Make-a-Wish Foundation. Most of all, fans have seen that no matter how many races Bill wins, he never loses his friendly, down-home smile. You can take the boy out of Dawsonville, but you can't take Dawsonville out of the boy.

Here is the smiling face of the most popular driver on the NASCAR circuit. Fans have named him their favorite an amazing 16 times!

MILLION DOLLAR BILL

In 1985, NASCAR drivers had a new trophy to shoot for. A large company put up a special prize of $1 million for any driver who could win all three of NASCAR's top races in one year. It was a long shot, but every driver wanted to take home that huge prize.

In 1985, Bill's long shot came in. The kid from Dawsonville won the first Winston Million by capturing the Daytona 500, the Winston 500 at Talladega, and the Southern 500 at Darlington. As he roared across the finish line at Darlington, he also earned a great new nickname, Million Dollar Bill.

16   The quiet before the storm: Here's Bill waiting for the start of the 1985 Southern 500. His win in this race would earn him a $1 million bonus . . . and a new nickname.

CHAPTER THREE

End of a Drought

Y ou'd think that a man who'd won 40 NASCAR races
would be pretty confident about claiming number 41.
But entering the 2001 season, Bill Elliott was anything
but optimistic.

Since taking the Southern 500 in 1994, he had strapped
on his helmet for 226 races—without a single victory. Think
of it this way. Bill's son, Chase, was six years old in 2001. He
had never seen his father win, not even as a baby. Sure, Bill
had come close. He was leading the last lap at Daytona in
1997 until Jeff Gordon, Terry Labonte, and Ricky Craven
ganged up on him. That race ended under **caution,** ruin-
ing Bill's chances to retake the lead.

Maybe Bill was overextended. In addition to his driving,
he had served as team owner since 1995. This was a

difficult job. There were times Bill would like to have been concentrating on driving. Instead, he had to worry about making his sponsor happy or keeping order among the crew members. It certainly didn't help his mental state when his father died in 1998.

Whatever the cause, Bill became as cold as a snowman. The guy who had dominated the sport for a decade finished 21st in the points standings in both 1999 and 2000. The low mark came in April 2000, when his sponsor, McDonald's, told him his contract would be dropped after the season. Bill was shocked. Money got so tight that crew members were sleeping on the floor of the race shop.

In 1999, Bill's sponsor plastered its familiar yellow initial on the hood of his car. Take a good guess at what his crew ate after races!

Then came a very important phone call. On the other end was Ray Evernham, who was well known as Jeff Gordon's crew chief. Ray has also been a popular broadcaster on ABC and ESPN. Ray had a new race team, and he wanted Bill to be his driver.

In some ways, the two men were opposites. Evernham is an easterner from New Jersey, known for being super-organized and very intense. Bill is pretty much a laid-back southern boy. But they had one thing in common: They loved talking about and tinkering with cars. So they joined forces, and Bill got behind the wheel of a Dodge Intrepid after 25 seasons driving cars made by Ford.

He knew he had a great team after testing in Chicago in 2001. Then he won the pole at Daytona—just like old times.

Teaming up with crew chief and car owner Ray Evernham gave Bill's career a big boost.

Still, he couldn't find that elusive checkered flag. "Ray and I have talked about it," Bill joked. "If we win a race, I may quit that day. It would be a good way to do it, say, 'I'm out of here, I'm done.'"

On November 11, 2001, the drought ended. The race was the Pennzoil 400. The site was Miami-Homestead Speedway. Bill Elliott was back in Victory Lane, and race fans were going crazy.

But Bill didn't quit as he had suggested. He had a feeling that big things were going to happen in 2002.

Earning a pole at Daytona, as this car did in 2001, is a team effort. Before Bill could drive his laps, his crew went over the engine carefully.

DRIVEN CRAZY

Talk about your big jobs. Dodge cars hadn't raced in the Winston Cup series in more than 20 years. But Dodge's parent company, DaimlerChrysler, decided to change that in 2001. They hired famous crew chief Ray Evernham to create an entire race program from nothing, using unproven cars.

Dodge designers worked with Ray and his team to craft a brand-new type of NASCAR vehicle. They were aided by computers and high-tech wind-tunnel tests. But Ray didn't get any computer help with the key member of the team.

He knew he needed a great driver, one who really knew his cars. So he hired Bill Elliott. Bill himself wasn't so sure it was the right choice at first.

"I thought maybe he needed a psychologist," Bill joked. "First for having a race team, and second for hiring me."

Dodge designers used high-tech computers and worked with Bill and Ray to create this state-of-the-art new NASCAR vehicle.

C H A P T E R   F O U R

Second Childhood

Everyone was talking about a new breed of NASCAR driver in 2002. There were several top young drivers such as Dale Earnhardt Jr., Jimmie Johnson, and Kurt Busch. But the biggest story of the year might have been a 46-year-old man in his 27th season of racing.

Awesome Bill from Dawsonville took three straight poles—at Talladega, California, and Richmond. He set a track record at Texas Motor Speedway while qualifying for the Samsung/Radio Shack 500, clocking a speed of 194.224 miles (312.57 km) per hour. And he made life a lot easier for the Evernham team.

"He has now really assumed the role as the team captain," Ray Evernham said. "He's keeping everyone else in check. He's making sure that we keep our feet on the

Still speedy in his 27th season, Bill set a speed record while qualifying for this race at Texas Motor Speedway in 2002.

Winner! Bill holds up the trophy he got for winning the 2002 Brickyard 400 at the famous Indianapolis Motor Speedway.

ground with the cars. He's the veteran quarterback." As for Bill, he said, "I'm having the most fun I've ever had driving a race car."

He seemed to be learning some new tricks, too. There was a time when Bill won races by simply driving harder and faster than anyone else. But it took more than a heavy foot to win the 2002 Pennsylvania 500 at Pocono Raceway, a grueling race that took eight hours from start to finish.

The race was delayed twice, first following a spectacular first-lap crash involving Earnhardt Jr. and Steve Park, and then because of rain. The rain delay forced drivers off the track for more than two hours. Worried about having enough daylight to finish, NASCAR officials notified teams on lap 125 that the race would be shortened to 175 laps. Bill nearly ran out of gas before making his final pit stop on lap 136. He passed Sterling Marlin with 18 laps to go and sped to victory.

A week later, he followed up his Pocono triumph by capturing the Brickyard 400 at Indianapolis Motor Speedway.

He led this one for 93 of 160 laps, driving his Dodge past Rusty Wallace's Ford with 12 laps to go. A caution flag signaled debris on the track, and the race restarted with only four laps remaining. But Bill blasted off on the restart. These were his first back-to-back wins in a decade (when he won four in a row in 1992), and they boosted him to the top 10 in the Winston Cup standings.

Two years earlier, Bill had been wondering if he should leave the sport of auto racing. Now he was eagerly looking ahead to the future.

"I'll eventually go by the wayside, and a new group will settle in," he said. "Nobody drives forever. But while I'm here, I'm going to do my best, work as hard as I can, and make the most of it."

And while every race season brings its surprises, some things never change. In December 2002, Bill edged Earnhardt Jr. to win the NASCAR Most Popular Driver Award. More than three million votes were cast by NASCAR fans. They showed, more than ever, that Bill Elliott is still America's favorite stock-car driver.

Though Bill Elliott has long been one of NASCAR's top drivers, he is looking forward to staying out in front—going as fast as he can!

STILL THE "BIG" KID

The stereotype of a race team might look a little like this. You'd have the gray-haired team owner who has spent years in the business. There would be a middle-aged crew chief with the wisdom of experience. Finally, you'd have a hot-shot young driver. But the Evernham team is pretty much upside down. Driver Bill Elliott is older than both owner Ray Evernham and crew chief Mike Ford.

At a press conference in Indianapolis in August 2002, Bill suddenly turned to Mike and said, "Tell 'em where you were when I won the championship in '88."

Mike looked bashful before replying, "I was still in high school."

Bill Elliott keeps the family racing legacy going by bringing his son Chase down to the track to watch his dad work.

BILL ELLIOTT'S LIFE

1955   Bill Elliott born on October 8

1976   Runs his first NASCAR race in a Ford Torino

1977   George Elliott buys racing equipment from Roger Penske

1981   Earns his first pole at the Rebel 500 at Darlington

1983   Harry Melling buys out George's racing operation; Bill wins the final race of the season, on a road course in Riverside, California

1985   On February 9, wins the pole at Daytona; wins a single-season-record 11 superspeedway races, including three that make up the Winston Million

1987   Records the fastest Winston Cup qualifying speed of all time, 212.809 miles (342.4 km) per hour at Talladega

1988   Is Winston Cup champion

1998   Named one of NASCAR's 50 Greatest Drivers of All Time

2001   Joins the Evernham race team and switches to a Dodge Intrepid; on November 11 breaks a 226-race winless streak with a victory at Homestead

2002   Wins back-to-back races at Pocono and Indianapolis and captures the Most Popular Driver award for the 16th time

GLOSSARY

bootleggers—people who carried or sold alcohol during the era of Prohibition, when it was illegal

caution—when an accident makes driving unsafe during a race, a yellow flag is waved and all drivers must slow to the same speed; no passing is allowed, and when the track is clear, the caution period ends and drivers resume racing

chassis—the steel frame of a car

checkered flag—black-and-white flag waved as the winning driver crosses the finish line

green flag—waved to start or restart a race

pole position—the first starting place in a race, usually on the front row closest to the inside of the track

restrictor plates—aluminum plates placed between the base of the carburetor and the engine's intake manifold, designed to reduce the flow of air and fuel into the engine

strategists—people who are skilled in making complicated plans

superspeedway—an oval, banked racetrack that is at least 2.5 miles (4 km) long

FOR MORE INFORMATION ABOUT BILL ELLIOTT

Books

Brock, Ted. *Fast Families: Racing Together through Life.* Excelsior, Minn.: Tradition Books, 2002.

McGuire, Ann. *The History of NASCAR.* Broomall, Pa.: Chelsea House Publishers, 2000.

Owens, Thomas S., and Diana Star Helmer. *NASCAR.* New York: Twenty-First Century Books, 2000.

Web Sites

Bill Elliott's Official Site
http://www.billelliott.com
To visit Bill's official site to read his comments about races, check out his fan club, and see action photos

ESPN
http://www.espn.com
For complete coverage of all NASCAR events from one of the nation's leading sports information providers

The Official Web Site of NASCAR
http://www.nascar.com
For an overview of each season of NASCAR, as well as the history of the sport, statistics, and a dictionary of racing terms

INDEX

Allison, Bobby, 9

Brickyard 400, 25–26
Busch, Kurt, 22

Craven, Ricky, 17

DaimlerChrysler, 21
Darlington Raceway, 9,
    16
Dawsonville, Georgia, 7
Daytona 500, 4, 16
Daytona Motor
    Speedway, 12, 19
Dodge, 19, 21

Earnhardt, Dale, Jr., 22,
    25, 26
Elliott, Bill
    in Brickyard 400,
        25–26
    charitable works of,
        15
    childhood of, 7–8, 12
    as Driver of the
        Decade, 14
    in Georgia Sports
        Hall of Fame, 13

as Most Popular
    Driver, 14–15,
    26–27
nickname, 4, 16
in Pennsylvania 500,
    25
in Pennzoil 400, 20
pole positions won
    by, 4, 19, 22
in Southern 500, 9
speed records, 6, 22
as team owner, 17–
    18
as Winston Cup
    champion, 12
in Winston Western
    500, 10
Elliott, Chase (son), 17
Elliott, Dan (brother),
    7, 11
Elliott, Ernie (brother),
    7, 10, 11
Elliott, George (father),
    7, 9
ESPN Speedweek, 14
Evernham, Ray,
    19, 21, 22, 28

Ford, Mike, 28

Georgia Sports Hall of
    Fame, 13
Gordon, Jeff, 17, 19

Hall, Roy, 7

Indianapolis Motor
    Speedway, 25–26

Johnson, Jimmie, 22

Labonte, Terry, 17

Marlin, Sterling, 25
Melling, Harry, 9–10, 12
Miami-Homestead
    Speedway, 20
Most Popular Driver
    Award, 14–15, 26–27

North Carolina
    Speedway, 8

Park, Steve, 25
Pearson, David, 9
Pennsylvania 500, 25

Pennzoil 400, 20
Penske, Roger, 9
Petty Richard, 15
Pocono Raceway, 25

restrictor plates, 6

Samsung/Radio Shack
    500, 22
Seay, Lloyd, 7
Sosebee, Gober, 7
Southern 500, 9, 16, 17
sponsors, 9, 18
Sports Illustrated, 13

Talladega Speedway,
    5–6, 16
Texas Motor Speed-
    way, 22

Wallace, Rusty, 26
Waltrip, Darrell, 4, 13
Western 500, 10
"Whiskey Trail," 7
Winston Cup Series,
    8, 10, 12, 16, 26
Winston Million prize,
    16

ABOUT THE AUTHOR

Phil Barber was an editor for NFL Publishing and is now a freelance writer. He contributes to several NFL publications and has covered football and other sports for *The Sporting News.* He wrote *The NFL Experience* and *Superstars of the NFL,* and co-wrote three other books. Phil has also written about the Daytona 500 and Dale Earnhardt Sr. He lives about a mile from Calistoga Speedway in California, so he can fill his need for speed easily!